FROM BEGINNING TO END

Painting Creation,

the Ten Commandments,

the Apostles' Creed,

and Apocalypse

ANNEKE KAAI

First edition, first printing
This edition © 2007 by Piquant Editions Ltd
PO Box 83, Carlisle, CA3 9GR, United Kingdom
Website: www.piquanteditions.com

ISBN-10: 1-903689-39-2
ISBN-13: 978-1-903689-39-4

The paintings from the 'Apocalypse', the 'Ten Commandments' and the 'Apostles' Creed' have been previously published in English as Anneke Kaai, *Apocalypse: Meditations on the Revelation of John in Word and Picture* (Carlisle: The Paternoster Press, 1992) and Anneke Kaai & Angela Taylor, *I Believe: Meditations on the Ten Commandments and the Apostles' Creed in Word and Picture* (Carlisle: The Paternoster Press, 1995). The 'Creation', 'Ten Commandments' and 'Apocalypse' series of paintings have been sold to private collections.

British Library Cataloguing in Publication Data
Kaai, Anneke, 1951-
    From beginning to end : painting Creation, the Ten Commandments,
    the Apostles' Creed, and Apocalypse
    1.Kaai, Anneke, 1951- - Themes, motives 2.Creation in art
    3.Ten commandments in art 4.Apostles in art 5.Apocalypse in art
    I.Title
    759.9'492

Cover Images © Anneke Kaai, 'Sun, Moon and Stars' (p18) and 'Alpha and Omega' (p84)
Design by Jeanette Obbink, Blueprint IT Works Inc.

Contents

4

About the Artist

Anneke Kaai-van Wijngaarden (b.1951) first studied art in the Netherlands at the Gooise Academie voor Beeldende Kunsten, where she had a classical training in drawing and painting. After that she continued her studies during the early 1970s at the Gerrit Rietveld Academie in Amsterdam. There she learnt to draw and paint in a completely new way, explored abstraction and developed a contemporary visual language. At the time she was moved by the emotional power of the Abstract Expressionists, but she did not share their life- and worldview.

Anneke's Christian faith runs like a golden thread through all her work. Her inspiration comes from meditating on and then giving expression to overtly biblical themes. Apart from the more figurative series on the Apocalypse, her work is abstract-symbolic: colour, form and line are all given symbolic values.

Anneke has completed six biblical series, namely 'Creation', 'Apocalypse', 'Ten Commandments', 'Apostles' Creed', 'Psalms' and 'Bible Words'. She is working on two further series—'Women of the Bible' explores the emotional lives of particular Bible characters, whereas 'In Relationship with God' expresses the gamut of emotions, from the very particular and extreme to the more common and general, experienced by Christians in their life with God.

Anneke always seeks new ways of picturing honest, passionate emotional realities—she searches out deep feelings and then struggles to make them felt. She paints increasingly in a more direct and spontaneous way. It is her challenge to engage the viewer in such a way that they too will experience, in their own way, something of the passion that inspires her personal faith in God.

Through her regular exhibitions in the Netherlands in churches of many different denominations, Anneke has played a role in bridging the divide that often separates the arts from church life. She has also held exhibitions in the UK and in Switzerland, and in 2005 and 2006 she presented her work at worship seminars in Grand Rapids in the USA.

This book makes Anneke's first four series of paintings available in print again: 'Creation', 'Ten Commandments', 'Apostles' Creed' and 'Apocalypse'. The 'Creation' series is here seen in an English edition for the first time. The artist's short descriptions and titles accompany the images. 'Psalms' and 'Bible Words' are available in print from Piquant Editions with accompanying texts by Eugene H Peterson as *The Psalms: An Artist's Impression* and *In a Word: See What You Believe*, respectively.

More information on Anneke Kaai's paintings and exhibitions is available on her website at www.annekekaai.nl

> *Great is the LORD and most worthy of praise; . . .*
> *One generation will commend your works to another*
> *. . . the glorious splendour of your majesty . . .*
> *And I will proclaim your great deeds.*
>   [Psalm 145]

Foreword

To Behold

One of my favorite words in the Bible is the slightly archaic term, 'behold'. It is a common English term to speak about how Old Testament worshipers related to God in the temple: 'One thing I asked of the Lord, that will I seek after: to live in the house of the Lord all the days of my life, to behold the beauty of the Lord, and to inquire in his temple' (Ps 27:4). The term also speaks of how God relates to us: 'The Lord is in his holy temple; the Lord's throne is in heaven. His eyes behold, his gaze examines humankind' (Ps 11:4). Even in the shadow of second commandment iconoclasm, Old Testament worship was an experience of 'beholding.'

The term implies more than simply viewing or listening or receiving something. It implies rapt attention and careful scrutiny. When we behold something, we not only perceive it, but we are taken by it. We are grasped by it.

'Behold' is the term I think of when encountering the works of Anneke Kaai. The works before you are works that evoke. They are mysterious, full of energy, marked by vivid contrasts and a vibrant palette. They invite you not simply to view them, but to see through them, to behold the wonder of the message they convey. In their own way, they teach lessons and narrate stories. But mostly, they inspire and evoke. They preach a little, but pray much.

Personal Prayer and Public Worship

Part of what makes this collection so valuable is that these works probe such central themes in the Christian faith. The opening and closing sections of this volume mark the grand movements of creation and new creation which frame a Christian worldview. The middle sections, based on the Ten Commandments and Apostles' Creed, convey the basis for both the ethics and doctrine of most Christian traditions. The Apostles' Creed—with its Trinitarian, narrative shape and extended Christological center—provides the Christological center to this book, and helps us perceive that this book is much like the Bible as a whole, with the life of Jesus helping us to understanding everything from creation to consummation.

As such, this volume is a sturdy primer for personal prayer. It is visual devotional, an artist's Book of Common Prayer. It will minister to visually-oriented people who have yearned for something beyond word-centered approach of most devotional resources. And it will challenge those of us who are not as visually-oriented to learn a new approach to prayer—prayer with our eyes open.

This work also has a significant potential for service in Christian worshiping communities. The past decade has witnessed both a profound recovery of arts as a vehicle of Christian expression and proclamation and the prodigious growth of new possibilities for artistic expression through computer projected technology (though many people who celebrate one of these developments are not as enthusiastic about the other!).

Consider ways that Anneke's work could help engage your community in the context of corporate worship. Consider projecting her work in lieu of other more pedestrian or mass-produced images.* Anneke's work can minister in this way because it is at once accessible to a wide range of people and substantially more nuanced and evocative than most readily available art on Christian subjects.

Most typically, this liturgical appropriation of her work would feature one image per service, chosen to correspond with the themes of the scripture readings, music, or sermon. Occasionally, however, something more elaborate is also possible. In a service in which Genesis 1 is featured (perhaps on a sunny Sunday in August for non-lectionary churches, or perhaps in an Easter Vigil for lectionary-based churches), consider projecting each of her creation images during a contemplative reading of the text. In a service in which the Apostles' creed is prominent, consider slowing down the recitation of the creed and viewing the sequence of her images as a visual accompaniment to the recitation. Each of these approaches will allow worshipers to sense the unfolding drama of both the texts and Anneke's commentary on them. By the power of the Spirit, these approaches may help worshipers move from merely hearing or reciting a text to beholding its meaning.

Eschatological Hope

Careful attention to this work may also help us experience one other sense of the term 'behold'. In some English translations of the Bible, behold also refers to an eschatological perception, to our experience of profound and confident hope.

Such is the sense of the enigmatic words of Numbers 24:17: 'I see him, but not now; I behold him, but not near—a star shall come out of Jacob, and a scepter shall rise out of Israel.' Somehow, the writer could behold the Messiah despite the distance of time and space.

Indeed, when Christians read the great eschatological promises of Isaiah 60 or 61 or Revelation 21 or 22, there is, in Christ, not merely a vague hope that these things will come about, but rather a quiet conviction that they will, as well as a profound longing for it to happen sooner rather than later. These promises offer us not merely the parched throat of our desert wanderings, but a foretaste of living waters of life. When these foretastes come through the Spirit, we, too, can behold the One who invites us to the heavenly feast.

My sense is that Anneke Kaai works as an eschatological painter. She tastes some of the drama and much of the goodness we anticipate in Christ. We, in turn, receive her work best by letting it stir up in us not merely appreciation for her form and style, but also deep longing for the goodness of the Lord. 'As for me, I shall behold your face in righteousness; when I awake I shall be satisfied, beholding your likeness' (Ps 17:15). May God's Spirit attend each of us as we encounter these works.

John D. Witvliet
Calvin Institute of Christian Worship,
Calvin College and Calvin Theological Seminary,
Grand Rapids, Michigan

*Note: Churches interested in projecting the images during public worship services should contact the publishers, Piquant Editions, through their website at www.piquanteditions.com for a CD-Rom with appropriate on-screen-use license agreement. The publishers are also happy to negotiate special bulk discounts with churches interested to buy multiple copies of this book for their members. Please read the copyright notice on p2.

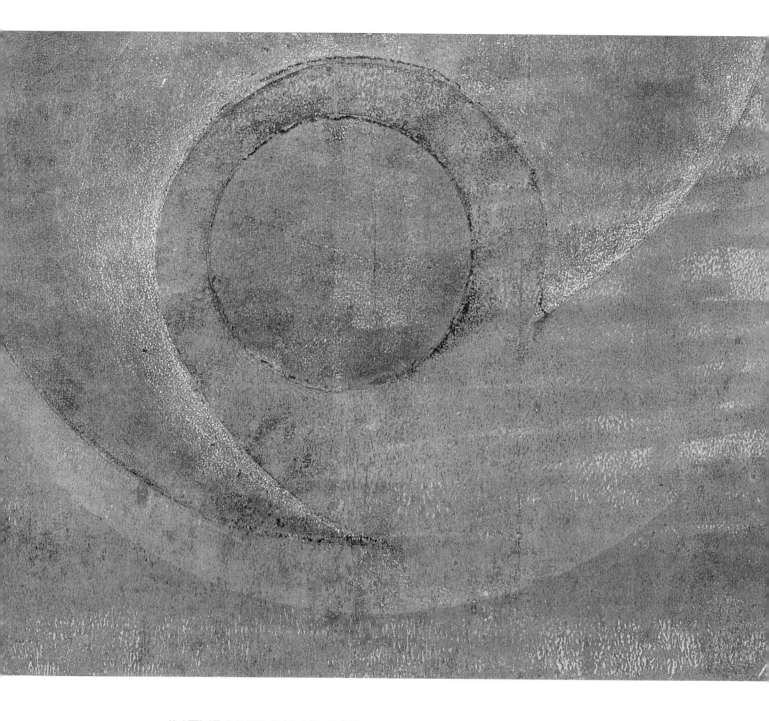

IN THE BEGINNING GOD …

God creates the heavens and earth. The heavens are vast: they embrace the small earth. The two belong together; they were created together.

CREATION (1986–88)

'In the beginning was the Word, and the Word was with God and the Word was God,' writes the Apostle John at the start of his Gospel when he reminds his readers of the beginning of all things in Creation. Anneke Kaai attempts to express something of the mystery and magnificence of Creation as recorded in the opening chapters of Genesis in her first fifteen paintings shown here. The sixteenth painting reflects God's amazing love for his creation as described in John 3:16.

The paintings are done in oils on a variety of mediums: paper or silk, sometimes in combination with collage. The original works vary in sizes of about 50cm x 40cm.

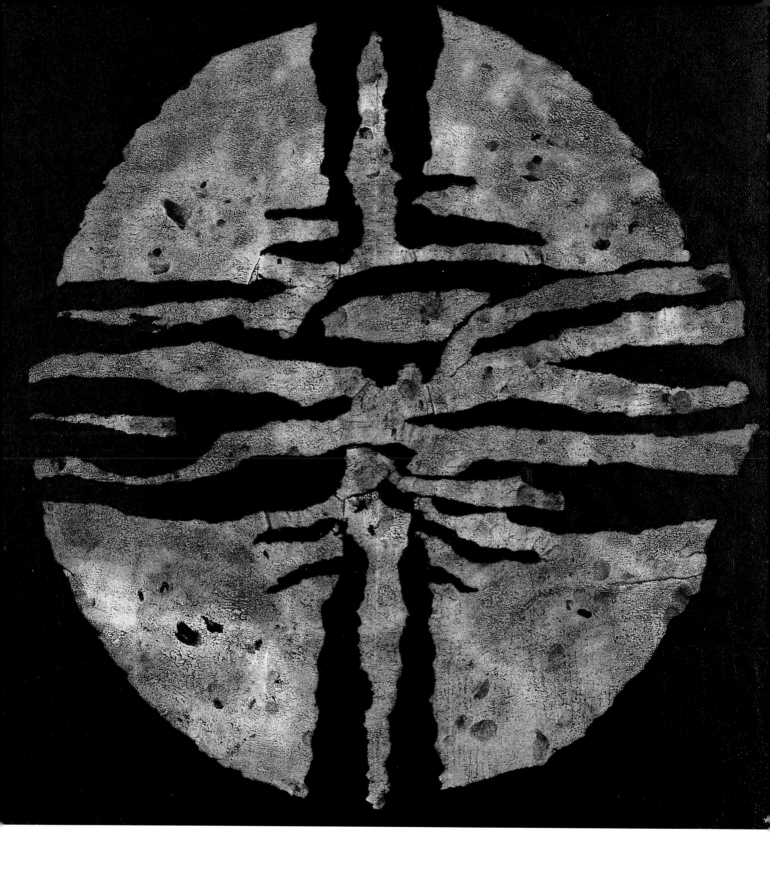

FORMLESS, EMPTY, DARK

God makes an earthly form take shape out of the desolate chaos and
darkness.

SPIRIT OF GOD OVER THE WATERS

Ruach Elohim hovers pregnantly over the unbridled
watery deep.

'LET THERE BE LIGHT'

God speaks. Mysteriously the darkness gives way to newborn light. It is the first morning.

DAY AND NIGHT

God separates light from the darkness; he calls the light 'day' and the
darkness 'night'.

WATER ABOVE, WATERS BELOW

God creates the sky above the earth. He separates the water above from the oceans below. The second day.

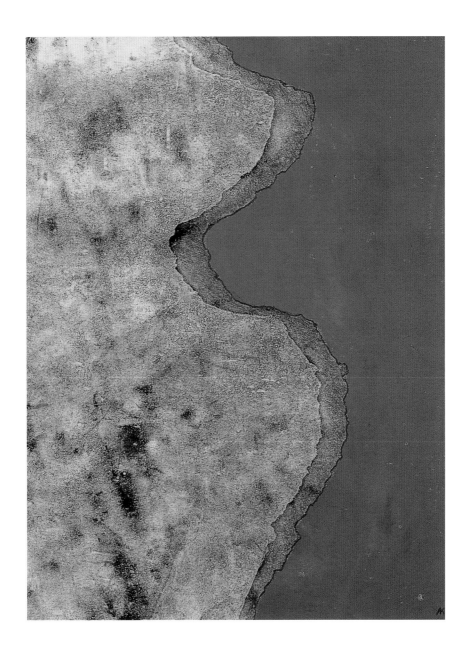

SEA AND DRY LAND

God makes the waters retreat. Dry land appears. The receding waters 'kiss' the land along the curving coastlines.

GREEN PLANTS AND VEGETATION

Out of the dark green, fertile earth young plants shoot up at God's command. They eagerly reach for the light.

> TREES, FRUIT, SEED

Each variety after its kind: God creates an abundant wealth of species, all jostling for space. The third day.

BIRDS AND FISH

God creates birds that fly, dive, swoop and glide in the sky, while fish populate the waters below.

SECRET CREATURES OF THE DEEP

Powerful, giant sea creatures move unseen along the silent, deep ocean currents. The fifth day.

LAND ANIMALS, WILD AND TAME

Livestock and wild animals lumber, frolic, skip and crawl across the dry
land: lamb alongside lion and crocodile.

'LET US MAKE "ADAM" IN OUR IMAGE'

To crown it all, God creates the first human beings: male and female, man and woman, a perfect match. The sixth day.

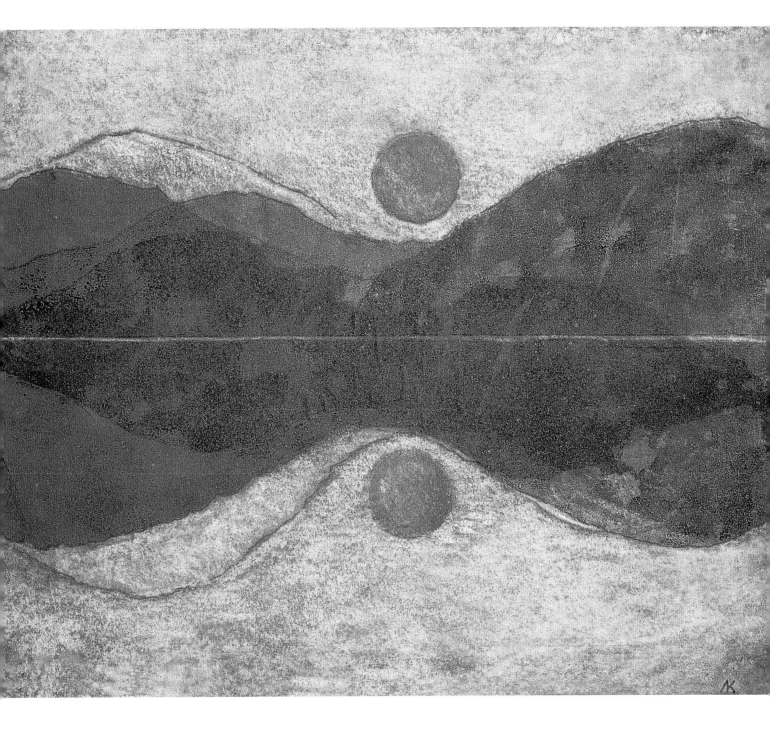

EVERYTHING IS VERY GOOD!

Perfect peace reigns as God evaluates his creation. Heaven reflects on earth.
God blesses the seventh day and rests.

FOR GOD SO LOVES THE WORLD …

Human sin spoilt God's perfect creation. And still we continue to tear it
apart. Yet the Cross embraces the scarred world: this is God's love!

THE TEN COMMANDMENTS
(1989–90)

The Ten Commandments, literally in Hebrew 'Ten Words', were given to Moses on Mount Sinai by God. The keeping of these rules would ensure lives of rich blessing and full joy for God's people. The first painting in this series expresses the context in which the Commandments were given: God had just rescued his people from slavery. The next ten paintings explore the meaning of each of the Commandments in a way that makes them applicable to life in the twenty-first century. The final painting expresses hope in God's provision of a way out for us who can never perfectly meet the requirements of his Law.

The paintings are done in oils on Plexiglas, all at size 60cm x 80cm.

I AM THE LORD YOUR GOD

The dark area at the foot of this painting refers to the Nile delta, where God's people had been slaves in Egypt. The silvery outline represents God's leading them from there to a fertile (green) land of promise (life).

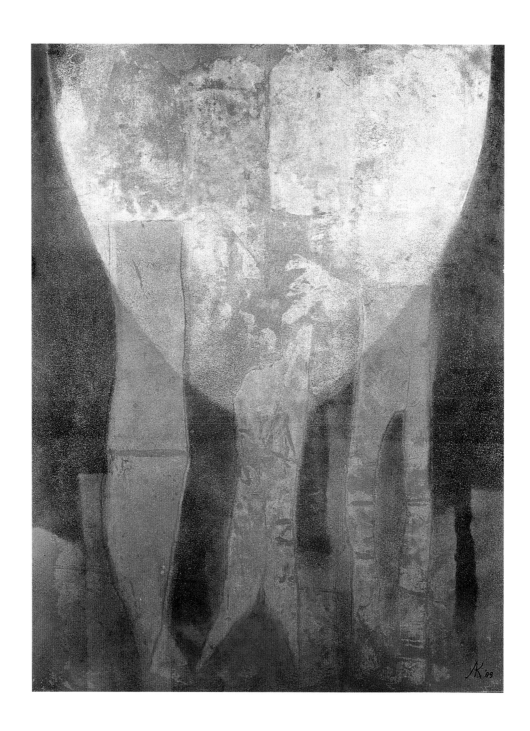

WORSHIP NO OTHER GODS

Other gods cloud our vision of the one true God. They seem to offer freedom but have no power and no substance, even when covered with gold. They pale in comparison with God. They cannot bring happiness.

> DO NOT MAKE OR WORSHIP IDOLS

God's people have been in contact with many idols. But God forbids (the broken idol) the making of any object to be worshipped, whether of something in heaven (white area above) or on the earth (green textured part of the sphere) or in the waters below (lower blue part of the sphere).

HONOUR GOD'S NAME

God's Hebrew name JHWH means 'I am'. It appears in the top left, light area of this painting. Below, in the dark area, the letters have been jumbled up. Red indicates the danger of misusing God's name.

> KEEP THE SABBATH HOLY

God instituted six 'regular' days for working. He demands that a seventh day be kept separate, free from such regular work, to be a special day for worshipping and honouring him.

RESPECT YOUR PARENTS

The Hebrew word for 'respect' literally means 'to make heavy'. We need to give our parents 'weight' as the bearers of God's Law, which they pass on to their children. Bright blue indicates God's faithfulness from generation to generation.

> DO NOT MURDER

This commandment does not refer to physical killing (long sword) only but also to 'killing' by the 'sword' of our tongues (right side) or through silence (the serpentine sword) and 'assisted' killing (the syringe-like sword). When all the swords are sheathed, inactive in the ground, the earth flourishes (light green background).

DO NOT COMMIT ADULTERY

God wants a couple to maintain their oath in marriage through love (red) and faithfulness (flecks of blue). Marriage also reflects the relationship between Christ and the church (interlocked cross and ring).

> DO NOT STEAL

All possessions are a gift of God (white area above). The wide golden track on the left represents the rich; the narrower, duller path on the right, the poor. A stolen portion never belongs to the thief, whether stolen from the rich or taken from the poor. It stays separated by a dark black area.

DO NOT TELL LIES ABOUT OTHERS

This commandment tells us to speak the truth (silhouette of the mouth on the right). When we distort the truth, we turn it upside down (dark silhouette on the left). What comes out of our mouths must be solid and straight (strip along the base of the painting).

> DO NOT COVET WHAT BELONGS TO SOMEONE ELSE

We lust after that which seems desirable (gold) to us. It is a powerful desire that is not easy to satisfy (red grasping hands). Red indicates danger. These restless desires will overcome us if we do not master them.

CHRIST FULFILS THE LAW

The cross of Christ embraces the two tablets of the Law. This painting radiates light, just as believers are to 'radiate' the good news that Christ died to satisfy the Law's demands. We follow him out of deep thankfulness.

THE APOSTLES' CREED (1990–92)

The twelve Articles of the Apostles' Creed are the most widely used formulation of the key beliefs of Western Christianity. They are the framework of many catechisms and informs the formal or informal liturgy of most denominations. The individual statements express deep truths in a direct and powerful way. Anneke Kaai grappled with abstract shapes to visualize the powerful emotions that accompany these bold affirmations.

The paintings are done in oils on Plexiglas, all at size 70cm x 100cm.

I BELIEVE IN GOD THE FATHER, CREATOR OF HEAVEN AND EARTH

God's fatherhood is represented by his embracing left arm (the white at the top of the painting). This shape is repeated in other paintings to communicate the same idea. With his right arm God creates the heavens and the earth, which is tiny in comparison to God's greatness.

> AND IN JESUS CHRIST, HIS ONLY SON, OUR LORD

There is a deep unity between the Father and the Son, expressed by the embracing arms of the Father that merge with the supporting arms of the Son. The Son is the mediator between the Almighty Father in heaven and human beings on earth.

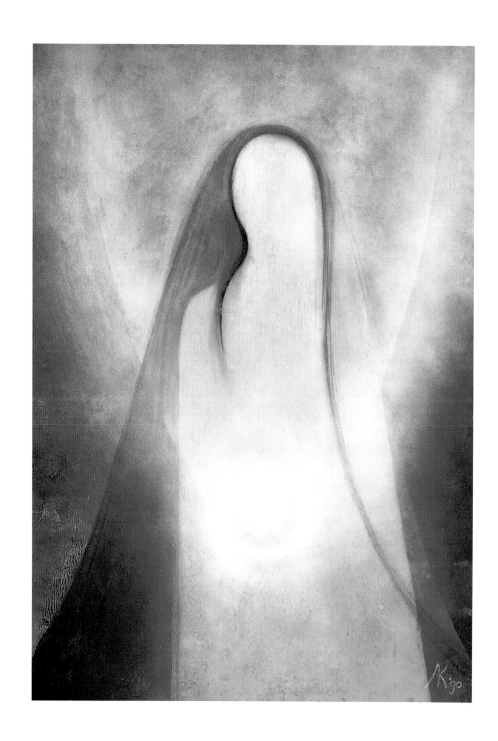

CONCEIVED BY THE HOLY SPIRIT, BORN OF THE VIRGIN MARY

The purity of Mary is clearly shown, as well as the overshadowing (white presence) by the Holy Spirit, who conceived the Holy Child.

> HE SUFFERED UNDER PONTIUS PILATE

The detail of the crown of thorns and the blood expresses the acute suffering of Jesus. The heavy dark grey area below reflects his utter loneliness and forsakenness.

WAS CRUCIFIED, DIED, WAS BURIED . . . DESCENDED INTO HELL

In this painting the composition is strengthened by a high horizon to emphasize the depth of suffering: 'My God, My God why have you forsaken me?'

> ON THE THIRD DAY HE ROSE FROM THE DEAD . . . ASCENDED INTO HEAVEN

The stone is rolled away (in the centre). Out of the dark depths of suffering (black area), Jesus is powerfully resurrected and ascends to the right hand of his Father (the light area above) in heaven.

WHENCE HE SHALL COME TO JUDGE THE LIVING AND THE DEAD

Shadowy light and dark figures, the living and the dead, are set against the background of life on the new earth (the light green colour). The old, fallen world shows to the right (dark side).

> I BELIEVE IN THE HOLY SPIRIT

By the Spirit's power, believers are carried along, 'set on fire' to become witnesses of the Cross and of the subsequent Resurrection of Christ.

I BELIEVE IN A HOLY CHURCH, THE COMMUNION OF SAINTS

The Cross of Christ is central, surrounded by the church of Christ, which is one body through baptism (blue) and the Lord's Supper (red) despite many divisions (torn shapes). The Cross also embraces the church, and the love of God surrounds and supports her.

I BELIEVE IN THE FORGIVENESS OF SINS

The red-and-black panel represents sin. It is in stark contrast to the visible part of the Cross, which covers the sin. The Cross is splattered with the blood of Christ.

> I BELIEVE IN THE RESURRECTION OF THE BODY

The natural, physical body is resurrected with immense energy into a glorified spiritual body. On the day of Resurrection, those who died in Christ will be like buds that open when they face into the bright sunlight.

I BELIEVE IN LIFE EVERLASTING!

The light path begins here on earth. There is no end to it as it disappears over the horizon into the light green new earth. It follows the curve of the Father's embracing arm: everlasting life is to be for ever in his care (the round shape represents eternity).

APOCALYPSE (1987–89)

The culmination of God's plan for this world is described in the last book of the Bible, the Apocalypse or Revelation of the Apostle John. After the opening two chapters, which contain letters to the seven churches in Asia, John describes a series of visions he received. Here Anneke Kaai portrays those visions in detailed figurative paintings to encourage readers to imagine the immense happenings described. The overall message of the Apocalypse is one of great hope: despite severe suffering, all things are heading towards a new heaven and earth where Christ, the victorious Lamb, is Lord!

The paintings are done in oils on silk at various sizes of about 50cm x 70cm.

< GOD UNVEILS HIS PLAN FOR THE FUTURE

The angel shows John what will take place in the future and commands him to write it down. Those who hear it and take it to heart will be blessed.

THE SON OF GOD WALKS AMONG THE SEVEN CANDLESTICKS

John sees a figure with hair like wool, feet like burnished bronze and a voice like the sound of rushing waters. He holds seven stars in his right hand. John recognizes Jesus and falls down as though dead.

> A DOOR IS OPENED IN HEAVEN: HOLY, HOLY, HOLY

A door in heaven is opened to reveal the throne of God, surrounded by twenty-four elders, four marvellous creatures, seven lamps and a sea of glass. The elders and the creatures are worshipping the One seated on the throne.

'WHO IS WORTHY TO BREAK THE SEALS AND OPEN THE SCROLL?'

An angel shouts. Then there is silence in heaven. Only one is found worthy to take the scroll and open its seals: he is the Lion of the tribe of Judah, the Root of David, Christ, the Lamb who was slain.

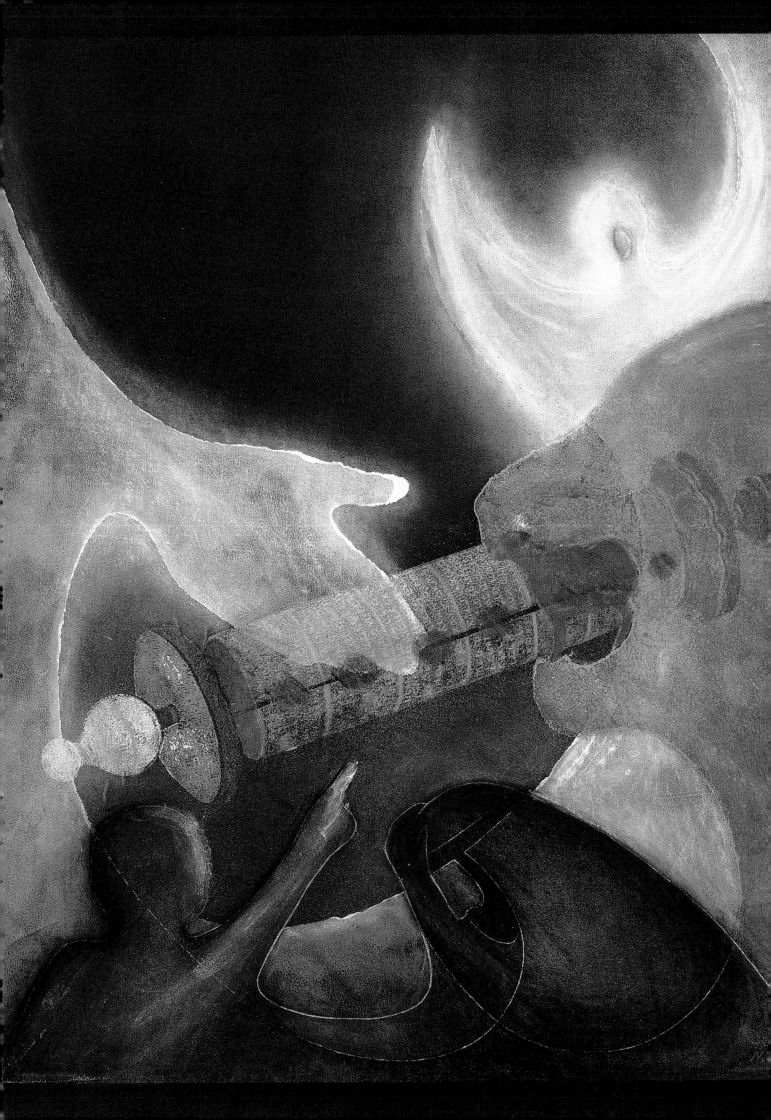

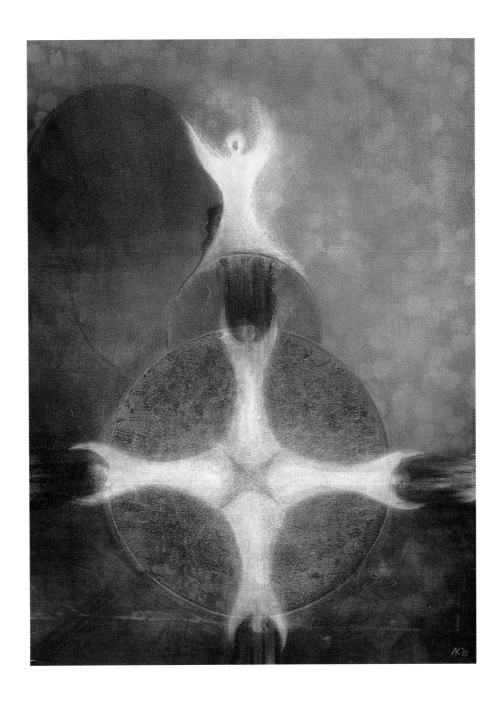

< SIX SEALS OF THE SCROLL ARE OPENED

The first four seals are opened to reveal four horses—white, scarlet, black and pale. The fifth seal reveals the altar in heaven and the souls of the martyrs. At the opening of the sixth seal the earth trembles and the sun is darkened.

∧ THE COMPLETE NUMBER OF ISRAEL ARE MARKED

Four angels at the ends of the earth hold back the storms. A fifth angel appears and receives a seal from God with which he goes about to mark (on their faces) the chosen ones of Israel.

A MULTITUDE GATHERS TO WORSHIP GOD

The heavens are filled with people. They come from all directions, from all nations and tribes. The number of those worshipping God and the Lamb cannot be counted.

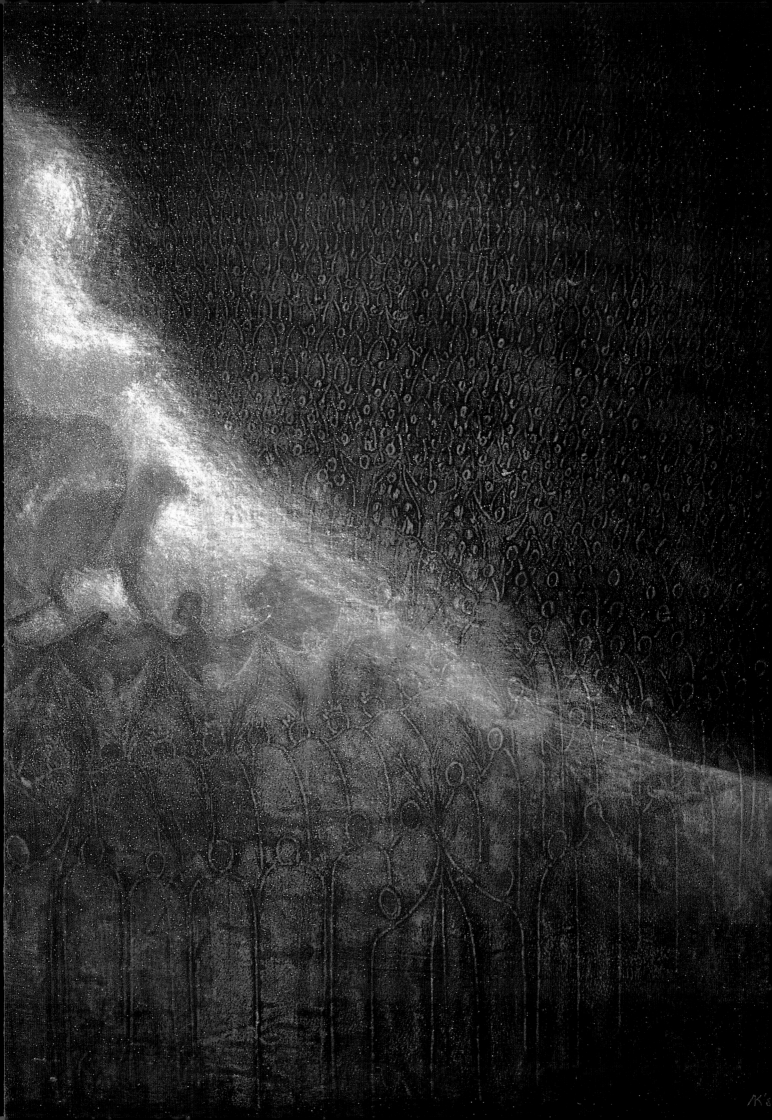

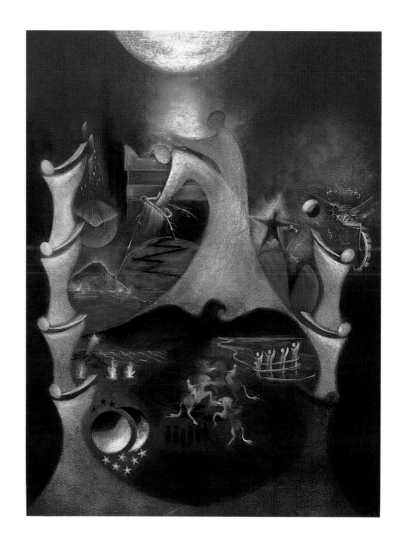

THE SIX ANGELS SOUND THEIR TRUMPETS

The seventh seal is opened by the Lamb. Then the six angels sound their trumpets, the sea turns to blood and wars break out. The earth is covered in fire, smoke and sulphur. (The message of the seventh, darker angel is still to be announced.)

> JOHN IS GIVEN A BOOK AND COMMANDED TO EAT IT

The mighty seventh angel is robed in a cloud and wearing a rainbow round his head. He announces the Day of the Lord and presents John with a small book, which he instructs John to eat in order to continue with his prophecy.

TWO WITNESSES IN BLACK SACKCLOTH PROPHESY

John is given a rod with which to measure the Temple, the altar and those who worship there. God sends two witnesses, who are killed by the beast from the abyss. When God's spirit enters the bodies of the witnesses, they arise and ascend to heaven in a cloud.

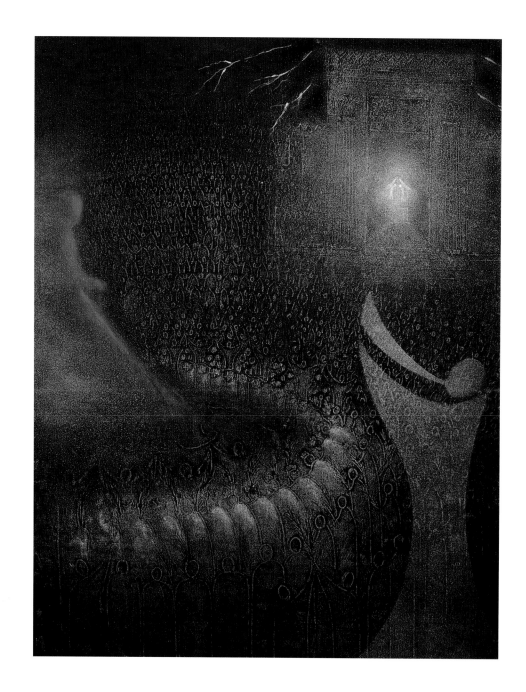

THE SEVENTH ANGEL SOUNDS HIS TRUMPET

The crowd cheers as God's eternal kingdom is finally established. The Temple of God opens up and the Ark of the Covenant is clearly visible to everyone amidst flashes of lightning and peals of thunder.

> THE WOMAN GIVES BIRTH TO THE CHRIST-CHILD

A woman appears, clothed with the sun. She cries out in pain and gives birth to the Christ-child, who is pursued by the red, seven-headed dragon. The woman escapes to the desert, while Michael and his angels hurl the dragon to the earth. The dragon tries to kill the woman with a powerful tidal wave, but earth swallows up the water. She lives.

THE DRAGON MUSTERS HELP

The dragon's helpers appear: a beast from the sea with seven heads and ten crowned horns and one from the land that looks like the Lamb (it is the beast of false prophecy). Those who worship the beast from the land receive its mark (on its body): 666.

> THE REDEEMED OF THE LAMB SING A NEW SONG

The Lamb stands on Zion's holy mountain. The 144,000 people who have been sealed follow the Lamb. They are the first fruits of the redeemed; they sing a new song, one that has never been heard before, a song that sounds like rushing water and the sound of many harps.

THE EARTH'S RIPE GRAPES ARE HARVESTED

Christ sits on a white cloud with a sickle, ready to collect the harvest. Three angels appear. The last one is instructed to gather the clusters of grapes. These sour grapes from the earth are thrown into the great winepress of God's wrath.

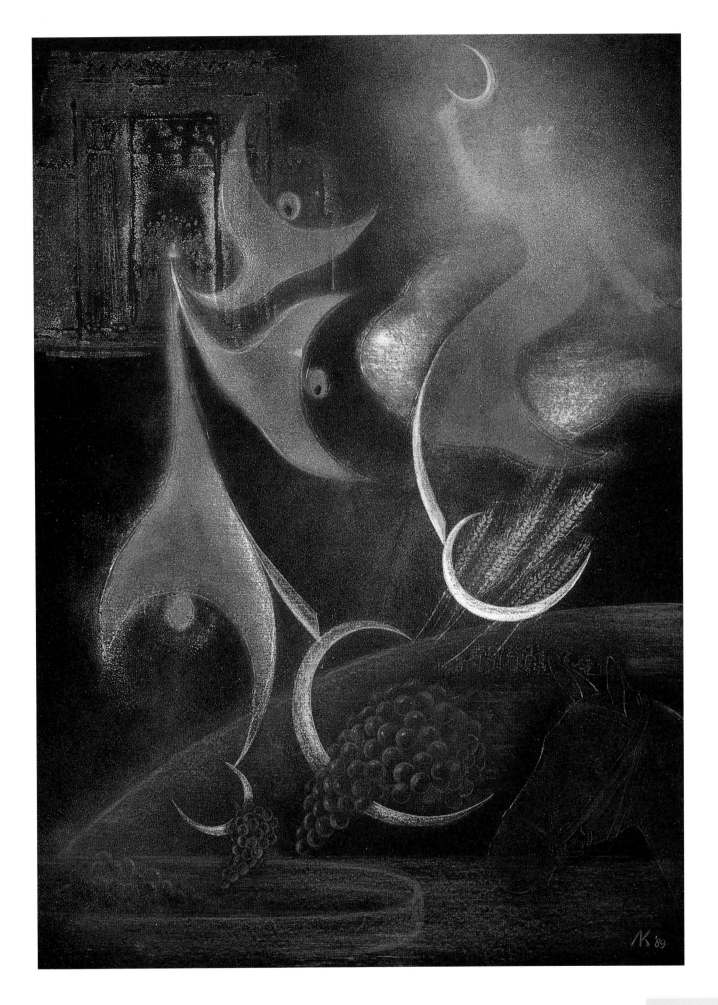

THE SEVEN ANGELS EMPTY THEIR SEVEN GOLDEN BOWLS

The seven angels pour out the bowls of God's wrath that they received from the four creatures. In the great battle of Armageddon the nations fight against the red dragon and his beasts (satanic frogs come from their mouths). The seventh angel pours out his bowl and proclaims: 'It is done!' The earth trembles and groans.

THE PROSTITUTE SITS ON THE BEAST: BABYLON FALLS

Babylon is the great prostitute, out to seduce the world for her master, Satan. She is drunk on the blood of God's witnesses. But the Lamb wins the battle, and the prostitute is burnt up, destroyed, never to be found again, lost like a millstone in the sea.

> KNIGHT FAITHFUL ON HIS WHITE HORSE DEFEATS THE BEASTS

Heaven opens up. The King of kings and Lord of lords wages war on the beasts from the sea and the earth and their scarlet armies. A white knight appears on a white horse. He throws the beasts into the eternal fire.

THE WEDDING OF THE LAMB IS CELEBRATED

A great multitude gathers. Their singing sounds like the roar of the waves.
It is the wedding of the Lamb and his bride, the church (a crowd forms her
dress). Blessed are those who are invited to the wedding feast of the Lamb!

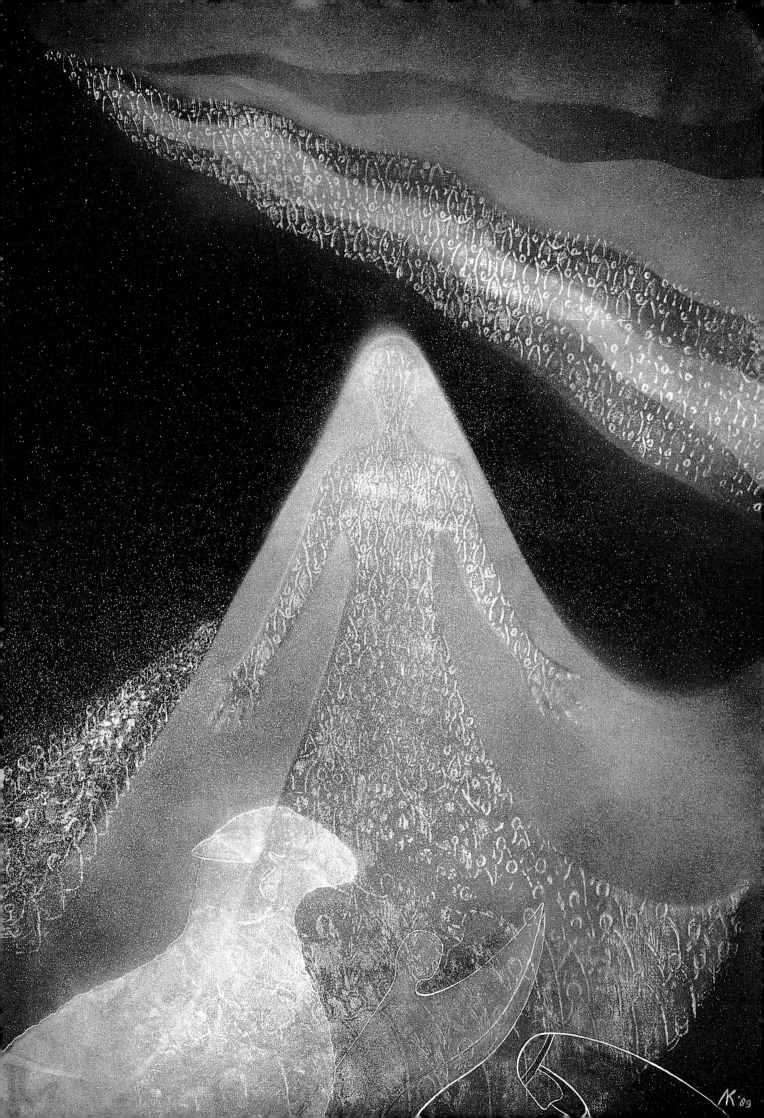

THE DRAGON SATAN IS IMPRISONED FOR A THOUSAND YEARS

The dragon is thrown into the abyss, where he is kept for a thousand years. When he breaks loose he attacks God's people. But God intervenes. The satanic dragon is thrown into the lake of fire that burns for ever (the same punishment that is suffered by his evil helpers).

> THE BOOKS ARE OPENED, ALSO THE BOOK OF LIFE

The dead from the sea and from Hades now gather before the white throne. The Book of Life and the other books are opened; they reveal everything. Then each person is judged according to the way they had lived.

THE NEW JERUSALEM DESCENDS

The angel shows John the New Jerusalem, the holy city, coming down from heaven. It is square and its foundations are precious stones. The streets are pure gold. Trees of eternal life grow along the banks of the river of living water. There is no Temple, no sun and no moon, because God on the throne and the Lamb are the light of this everlasting city of peace.

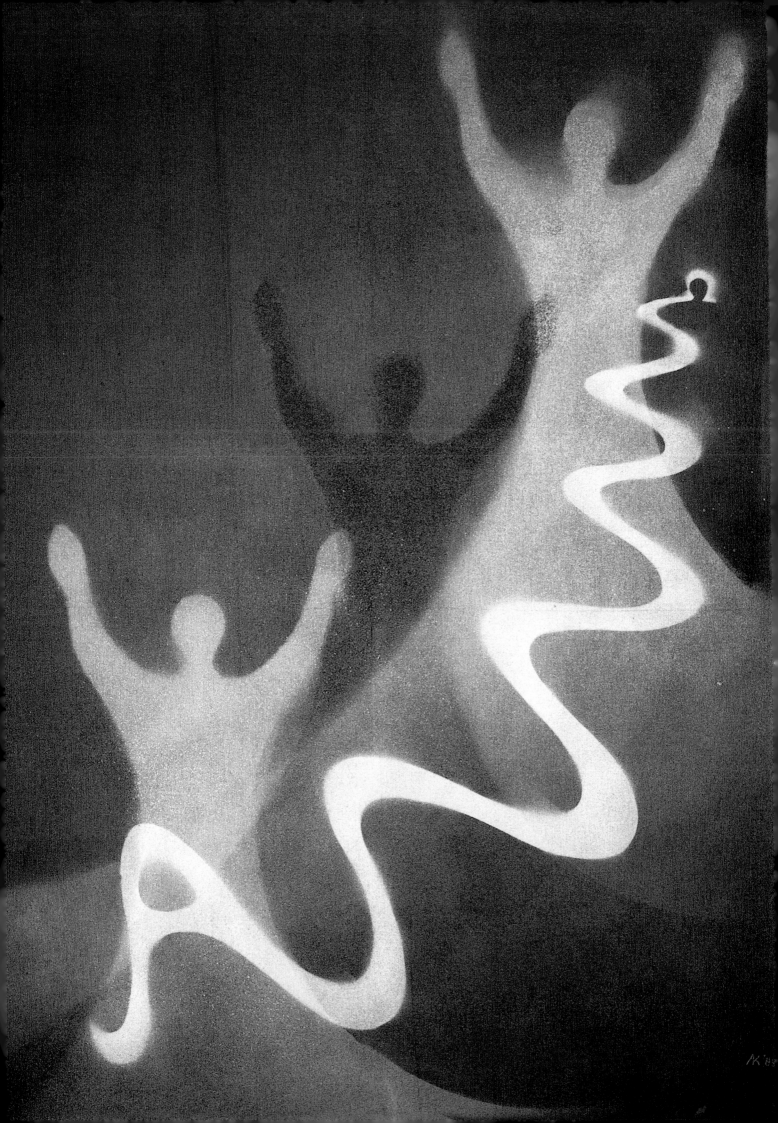

< ALPHA AND OMEGA

The One who is the beginning and end of everything, the first and the last, the Almighty One, he is the Lord of all!

∧ AMEN. COME, LORD JESUS!

Jesus is the bright Morning Star. Though at times it may seem as if clouds hide him from our sight, he remains faithful. He will reveal himself on the Day of the Lord.

Image List & Bible References

IN THE BEGINNING

THE TEN COMMANDMENTS

THE APOSTLES' CREED

APOCALYPSE

* For visual impact, the images on pp77 & 79 appear in reverse chronological order.